DEDICATED
TRANSPORTATION MANAGEMENT

DEDICATED TRANSPORTATION MANAGEMENT

Christopher Ackiss

Tampa, Florida

The views and opinions expressed in this book are solely those of the author and do not reflect the views or opinions of Gatekeeper Press. Gatekeeper Press is not to be held responsible for and expressly disclaims responsibility of the content herein.

Dedicated Transportation Management

Published by Gatekeeper Press
7853 Gunn Hwy., Suite 209
Tampa, FL 33626
www.GatekeeperPress.com

Copyright © 2022 by Christopher Ackiss

All rights reserved. Neither this book, nor any parts within it may be sold or reproduced in any form or by any electronic or mechanical means, including information storage and retrieval systems, without permission in writing from the author. The only exception is by a reviewer, who may quote short excerpts in a review.

Library of Congress Control Number: 2022947262

ISBN (paperback): 9781662933516
eISBN: 9781662933523

THIS BOOK IS DEDICATED TO:

The people who gave me the most leeway in running their businesses. Also, Tammy A. and the children, as they lived through all the seventy-hour work weeks and failed engagements. For that I am deeply sorry.

PREFACE

This book is my attempt to reach a group of transportation professionals who have questions about how to manage their operations. In my opinion, there is really a very limited amount of information published on how to manage dedicated transportation operations: the nuts and bolts of making the seemingly simple, yet very complicated, dynamics of a distribution center work efficiently. To most people, it is just, "the transportation department." They can solve all the problems by pushing the problems out of the system, and then tomorrow, if not repaired or fixed, you will have the same issue. How do you take these chronic issues and make them a "win-win" for the customer and the business? Well, you fix the larger problems within the operation that are really costing you or your firm a lot of money. Then the small things that you do become just that, small things that improve customer satisfaction without breaking the bank. You manage day-to-day events rather than wonder, when the P&L is out of alignment, why it is that way. You can explain with confidence why transportation costs have spiked and that everything is under control. I sincerely hope that this book will be able to help you and your firm regain control of your business and your seventy-hour work weeks and give you back some of your life.

TABLE OF CONTENTS

Preface vii
What Is It? 1
Parts and Terminology 2
Dispatch 3
Routing 5
Routing Tactics 6
Driver Work Schedules 7
Route Optimization 8
Driver Route Optimization 8
Extra Board Creation and Utilization 11
Tractor Assignments and Utilization 11
Managing Cost 12
Manager Responsibilities 14
Addressing Problems 14
Management of the Entire Business 16
Distribution Center LTL Program 17
Setting Up Distribution Center Inbound Backhaul Program 18
On-Site Fueling 19
Advanced Extra Board Utilization 20
About the Author 23

DEDICATED TRANSPORTATION

What Is It?

What is dedicated transportation? That's a good question. First, let's identify other modes of transportation so that it all makes sense. There are a host of different modes that people work in; brokerage, export, import, domestic, air, rail, LTL, inbound or traffic, outbound and shipping, and there may be more. This just a partial list. All of these are modes or functions, types of transportation that people work in, as well as dedicated—which is a group of drivers, trucks, and trailers assigned to a location. In most cases, these people and equipment would be assigned to a distribution center or a manufacturing facility and support their operations to get their products to their customers. They may also aid in getting raw materials, or inputs for distribution or manufacturing, back to the facility. "Dedicated" is the term that describes these activities because the equipment and drivers are assigned to the facility.

If your staff pulls orders or builds something that goes on a truck for delivery (either directly or from storage), this information can help you navigate and manage your facility. It will also hopefully give you ideas about how to improve any problem areas of your operation.

Parts and Terminology

The word "parts" refers to the different pieces of equipment and people—things that blend together to make up a dedicated operation. The first is a truck, tractor, day cab, sleeper unit, and power unit. All of these are the same thing, with the exception of the sleeper unit, which is a truck with a bunk for either a single driver or a team of drivers to manage HOS (hours of service) without needing to find a hotel. Second, the next part which connects to the tractors is the trailer. The terminology for these, like the tractor, varies. They can be called a host of things. Here are some examples. Dry van (twenty-six, thirty-two, forty-eight, or fifty-three feet in length) are some of the most commonly used variations, or a trailer referred to as a "reefer" unit, which is a trailer with a cooling unit on it. These typically come in either a single-stage cooler or split wall with a freezer and refrigerator. Another would be the pup combo, typically in the south called a "double set" or in the north run as "triples." These are two or three twenty-six foot trailers tethered together with a piece of equipment known as a "converter dolly." The converter dolly can be referred to by different names, including "Joe dawg," "dawg," or "dolly." Also, sometimes a pup trailer can run single to utilize fewer cubes for small deliveries and enhance the turning radius for places that are difficult for larger equipment to get into. So, we have a truck, a trailer, and a converter dolly, and now for the fourth, or last piece. This would be a "straight truck." A straight truck comes in several different lengths; the most common is a twenty-six foot box truck. This piece of equipment consists of a power unit with a connected trailer and no converter dolly. The unit is all built together and, in some cases, can have both a reefer unit and sleeper unit attached. They typically are used for small expedited deliveries up to about 12,000 lbs. for local deliveries and pickups. This type of unit gives the company flexibility over the equipment.

Dispatch

"Dispatch" is a function, or place when and where drivers are either pre-scheduled or dynamically scheduled. They come to the distribution center or facility, and they receive their daily work assignment from a person called a "dispatcher."

A dispatcher does a multitude of things; for instance, they assign trailers and tractors to drivers. Dispatchers track equipment that is OOS (out of service), in the shop, or otherwise not available for use, aka "red-tagged." Dispatchers also route, in most cases, the deliveries going on the trucks. Dispatchers also keep track of where drivers are located. The reason for this is so that, if for some reason the driver cannot make their next dispatch, the driver is taken off the dispatch or moved to a later run when they will be available. Dispatchers also give out paperwork to drivers when they "dispatch" them. When the drivers return from the route, the dispatcher collects from the drivers's all of the appropriate paperwork and the POD (proof of delivery) is signed and accounted for. When the dispatcher is checking in the driver, if the POD is not present, they will question where the paperwork is and why it was not present or signed for and returned and where the freight is. This is a big responsibility because it ensures the company has proper documents to get paid by the company to whom they sold the goods.

Routing

"Routing" is the process by which the orders for the facility come in and are assigned a truck by geographic region and set up for delivery. There are lots of things that occur during the routing process for the dispatcher. Orders can be downloaded from a server into the routing software. This is called "dynamic routing." In some cases, a listing of routes is provided by an internal IT department that runs a report with the routes for the day and all the orders that have come in. This is typically called "static routing." In either case, the purpose of this exercise is to make sure that all the deliveries will fit on the truck they have been assigned to. If, by chance, the deliveries will not fit, they will need to be reassigned. The cubic volume, also known in the industry as "cube," and the weight of the product are the two measurements that determine what is going to go on the truck, or trailer in this case. Typically, with a combined gross weight of 80,000 lbs., this is the legal weight of the truck, trailer, and weight of all the deliveries.

Routing Tactics

The layover-load split: This is a tactic where you have a load on a trailer that has a two-day delivery route. The load will not fit on the truck, so you break it at the layover. The primary driver can come back from his first day and then dispatch out on the second day after returning home for his break, or you can, if in a remote area, shuttle the layover to him or have a second driver just deliver the route on the next day. There are multiple things you can do in this scenario. If you shuttle the second day to the primary driver, the shuttle driver, after swapping trailers, can go and get a backhaul or inbound load before returning to the DC or facility.

The route-building split: For this tactic, you take an overly large route and break part of it off, leaving the primary driver or drivers a full trailer and creating a second load with a later dispatch time. You could then build a route with stops from other trucks that are over capacity, and this would minimize the impact on the warehouse.

The stop-moving dynamic: In this tactic, you would take an overly large truck and move selected stops off the truck to a truck that has the capacity and can deliver within the approximate pre-planned delivery time. If the delivery time varied, you would put together a call sheet on all the stops that had variations, call them one by one, and give them their new ETA.

Driver Work Schedules

Driver work schedules, or delivery route schedules, should be put together by the company's management team, or with the help of senior drivers. This would preset the hours for each driver to work for each week and miles per driver. There are several ways to parcel out the work schedules. The one I used in the past the most was longevity with the company. This is a rewards system. The drivers get to pick their work based on the theoretical pay of the work schedule, and they schedule when they want to work for an indefinite period. If you don't have a lot of variation, perhaps you run the schedules for the entire year. If you have quite a bit of variation, maybe you re-route and optimize two times a year. It will depend on your individual business, and the volume swings or patterns your business is susceptible to.

Route Optimization

"Optimization," "right-sizing," or "re-routing" are terms used to describe the process of re-evaluating the routes that are currently being run or dispatched. Over time, routes get new stores or deliveries added to them, and the routes grow, which causes them to no longer be optimal. I like to go to a conference room, hook my computer up to a video projector, and throw the routes up on the wall to look for overlapping and crisscrossing of routes. Reviewing low-volume routes and stop and cube averages provides data for shifting stops around until the cube, mileage, and weight of each route is ideal. This is optimization, or re-routing.

Driver Route Optimization

The first thing you will want to do is take all your loads that your facility runs for outbound Sunday through Saturday, all seven days, and throw them up on the wall, figuratively, not literally, and see where they land. You will need to document each load; I suggest using a piece of paper for each load, hours, return time, stops, destination and dispatch time, and route number.

	Sunday	Monday	Tuesday	Wednesday	Thursday	Friday	Saturday	Miles	Hours
1	Off	rt 1 0500 25 hours 725 miles	deliver	return	rt 10 0500 12 hours 525 miles	rt 16 0500 10 hours 250 miles	Off	1500	47
2	rt 2 1000 25 hours 900 miles	deliver	return	rt 7 1000 14 hours 475 miles	rt 15 1100 7 hours 250 miles	Off	Off	1625	46

You will want to grid out your runs. This method is the way you are throwing these up against a wall, with a column for miles and total hours on the right. See the example above. You will be able to see the total hours drivers are working, potential HOS issues, route coverage issues, and potential deficiencies where drivers could be doing more or less work. You will take route #1 from Monday's dispatch sheet and place it on your diagram (spreadsheet) and then a Tuesday route that will fit in with a like dispatch time. This is the process of building a work schedule for your group of drivers—an analysis of what you think your ideal would be. You can also do this with your current work schedules and put them side by side to see where your inefficiencies lie.

DEDICATED TRANSPORTATION MANAGEMENT

Once you have all your routes diagrammed out, you will number each of the route groupings as one, two, three, etc. Whatever you have, this will tell you how many drivers you will require for the new route groupings. If you end up having too many drivers for all the new route groupings, create your extra board with those drivers who are extra. This "extra board" is discussed in another section below.

Extra Board Creation and Utilization

An "extra board" is a concept where you hire or have "extra" company drivers at the facility. Typically, this is comprised of 10% of the total driving force of the facility. So, you have 100 drivers your extra board would be comprised of ten drivers. These drivers do extra work, and vacation or sick time coverage, etc. If a driver calls off in the middle of the night, you call the extra board to cover the work. This math is by no means the end all be all. It is just a guide for where to start. Depending on the depth of your driving force, you might need fifteen extra board drivers. But the expectation is that you will be tracking load splits on a daily basis and building new route schedules for the drivers out of these splits.

Tractor Assignments and Utilization

"Tractor utilization" is just what it implies. Tractors are assigned to drivers by mileage of the route and mileage on the unit. Newer units are placed into a grouping for the longer routes to pick or be assigned from, and older units are kept closer to the facility, so breakdowns don't keep drivers out overnight, and such things can be repaired or towed at a quicker response time and less expensively.

Managing Cost

Manager and router/supervisor responsibilities:

- Manage your routes every day
- Manage average cube
- Manage driver scheduling
- Manage your backhaul program
- Manage on-time deliveries

Managing the routing is a day-to-day job. This is not just true for the supervisor doing the routing but also for the manager of the facility. The manager and the supervisor must work together to question routing scenarios and best practices to get out of your routing software the best possible routes to maximize cube and or pallets per dispatch.

Cube: Keep your trucks full. Full trucks pay the bills. Get those unnecessary trucks off the road, and reduce your cost and accident potential. A truck on the road is a liability. A truck with several stops on it that could have been on another truck is an expense and accident waiting to happen.

Review your driver scheduling daily to make sure everyone is being used effectively. Utilize as many company drivers as possible if you are using temps in your operation and do everything possible to reduce temps and hire permanent drivers. Make sure the names on the dispatch are solid and not just a name to say the work was done. Create effective methods of tracking drivers, so you know where they are, and so does your staff. This is important to the business and the families whose family member works for you. An employee and their family feel discontent when they are called to come to work at night and the employee is on a previous route layover.

Push customer service from your drivers and on-time deliveries. This keeps the customers happy. Happy customers mean that drivers come and go with ease at the delivery, keeping trucks on time. Phone calls continually from customers that are looking for trucks or having delivery issues are not issues that you should be having, and they are not productive. Solve the problems by working with the driver, and if necessary, go visit the customer. If you follow these simple guidelines, you should have a productive, profitable operation with happy long-term employees.

Manager Responsibilities

Review your payroll weekly, even if you pay biweekly. This reduces the amount of time you have to spend on this process at payroll close. You cannot catch everything, but scrutinize to eliminate issues. Nothing will sour the morale or confidence in you in your operation faster than employees thinking you are messing with their pay.

Manage your budget daily. Set up a spreadsheet with your variable cost items and monitor them as you pay the bills—tires, maintenance, fuel bills, parts, windshields, mud flaps, and bumpers. If you track, measure, and reduce waste, you should make your budget if it is written correctly, and you will be able to explain your misses.

Addressing Problems

- P&L issues (triage the department)
- Staffing is an issue.
- Logging/route issues/warehouse

First, no one is going to help you; let's just make that clear right up front. You have been chosen as the person with the most skills, knowledge, and work ethic to lead your department. You must assess the department thoroughly, like medical triage. Determine through your profit and loss which part of the department is broken, fixable, or stable. I am kind of a top-down person, so

I typically start with staffing. In the beginning, determine with the current situation how many drivers it takes to operate effectively. Then go on a campaign to add at least five more drivers than you think you need. Over hire as they will not all stay, and you do not want to continually be working on this part of the equation. Then once you have the hiring in place, HR can support you by getting in the drivers, and you can start to focus on fixing the other problems you may have. Make sure everyone is legal, taking the appropriate breaks, getting back from their routes on time, and that the warehouse is dispatching loads on time as well. They are built and completed on schedule for the drivers to leave at the designated time. Nothing kills drivers' hours of service more than standing around waiting on a route. They are getting paid, and typically they don't want to be waiting. Drivers want to drive. You will turn over all the drivers you just hired if you do not fix the issue. Create the extra board if it does not exist. This should be first and foremost, and all the drivers that you hire initially will go straight to this driving position.

These moves should stabilize the business so that you can follow the outline of this text. Start in the beginning. First, make sure your router is getting routes to the warehouse production floor on time. If the floor is not starting on time, this must be fixed; it is part of your problem. Review and optimize driver schedules. Then you're routing tractor assignments; create the backhaul program after the department is stabilized and running smoothly.

Management of the Entire Business

- *Warehouse Balancing:*
  What exactly does "balancing a warehouse" mean? Exactly what it says, you shift (product/case count/deliveries/volume) from over-productive days to less-productive days to balance the workload across all operating days. This is accomplished by changing delivery days for customers from one delivery format to another. For example, you move one-day-a-week deliveries to all-Wednesday deliveries to build volume here because you have one-day-a-week stores on Monday and Friday, creating unnecessary extra volume on days where you are already busy. You do this across all operating days so that the case count per day for selection is "balanced."

- *What this does for the operation:*
  This process allows the warehouse management team to effectively schedule labor and budget labor across the warehouse enterprise and eliminate spikes in staffing daily for picking and loading crews to control overtime. This process also allows trucks to be completed on time, eliminating the driver hours issue of sitting and waiting for loads to be ready, and customers get their deliveries on time. If you re-route periodically for summer and winter volumes, this should also be part of the process.

Distribution Center LTL Program

This is a process that can reduce traffic on your yard, non-employees on your dock, and save a little money on inbound that is not backhauled but comes in on LTL (less-than-truckload) carriers. First, get with your purchasing department buyers. Coordinate with them to reduce the number of LTL carriers to maybe two. Then once your team has made a choice about which carriers you will approach, call the salesperson for the carrier to come by and see you to negotiate your discounted freight rate. Essentially what you are going to do is drop a trailer at their terminal, and when they have your inbound, they will load all the freight on your trailer, and you will schedule a driver daily to go pick up this trailer and drop another empty. The driver will bring all the freight back to the center to be received and put away by the DC. The buyers will specify either of the LTL companies when they buy so that all the freight is channeled into them. You then get a great price, you keep all the LTL carriers off your lot, and your inbound is not tied up waiting to be delivered.

DEDICATED TRANSPORTATION MANAGEMENT

Setting Up Distribution Center Inbound Backhaul Program

A backhaul program is a process where trucks that work for a dedicated fleet stop, once empty, to pick up freight destined for the DC. The transportation manager or dispatcher meet with the buying group on a predetermined day every week. The transportation staff and the buying group discuss what can be picked up on the company trucks versus shipping third party. The dispatcher then accepts the loads for his trucks that are empty and passing through on the way home. This way, the cost is minimal to the company.

This freight is most likely either truckload or small quantities of goods (several pallets) that will be sold and go back out for deliveries. Set up a goal on how much freight you would like to attempt to get and work towards the goal. Since the company has an empty truck rather that pay to ship, you as the manager or dispatcher use your truck and have the driver stop by, pick up the freight, and bring it back to the DC. The transportation department receives an allowance, predetermined by accounting, for the cost of the freight being picked up, and they use or apply this money to the P&L as a credit. This reduces the overall cost of doing business.

On-Site Fueling

This section is for DC operators that have fueling stations, tractors, or reefer trailers. If your fuel is contracted, you can still save money. Fuel is purchased on the open market, and prices move up and down daily. These swings are big some days, other times not so much. But you are hopefully buying 8,000-8,400 gallons at a time, so if you save ten cents a gallon several times a month, you could be talking about substantial savings. Fuel prices change at 6:00 p.m. daily after the market closes. So, prices before 6:00 p.m. are one price (previous days close after 6:00 p.m.), and prices after 6:00 p.m. daily are another price. Also, there is rack pricing. The rack is the vendor: Valero, Kinder Morgan, Marathon, etc. So, you always want the lowest rack possible and then the pricing either before or after 6:00 p.m., if you can stand to wait for fuel to be delivered. Sometimes the prices after 6:00 p.m. go up depending on the close.

Advanced Extra Board Utilization

So, you want an extra board. Great news: we can help you set one up! As discussed in the section on Extra Board Creation and Utilization, you will need to know as the beginning total number total numbers of drivers. Just as an example, for every 100 drivers you would need ten seats on the extra board. This number can greatly vary depending on load splits, length of service, vacation, and personal days employee's take. But this is, as I mentioned, a good place to start. Also, the extra board is a great place for new drivers to start during the year. As they run and learn the routes you will have a seasoned driver force who knows the routes come route selection time. They will be able to make informed decisions about their work for the next six months or longer.

Step 1. Either with a spreadsheet program, or on a piece of paper, diagram out for one week all the drivers the company will have off work. This would be PTO, vacation, etc. and going forward you will need to set up a tracking mechanism for this, if you don't have one already, when vacations and personal days are approved.

Step 2. On this piece of paper typically you will need to list your 10% of drivers that do not have work in some numerical order.

Step 3. Go down the list and ask the first driver what he would like to do for the following week. Pencil in that work by his name and simultaneously take the work off the available work list. This work is covered. Repeat this process until all planned unscheduled work has a driver assigned to it.

Doing this process daily and weekly will ensure that loads don't sit on the yard and all your commitments to customer deliveries are taken care of.

Step 4. The drivers who do not have work will be your fill-in drivers for the week. This means that these drivers will cover call-ins (not planned), sick days (not planned), and load splits (as discussed in routing tactics).

Step 5. For team routes that have one driver off, the senior driver is the one who is not taking the day off and second seat is the fill-in driver. Routes with one driver you can decide if someone on the extra board knows the route and hopefully staff it that way with that driver.

Driver 1	Rt. Pkg.	S	M	T	W	Th	F	S
Tommy	pkg 3 seat 2	Off	M101	d/r	WD303	d/r	F505	d/r
Michael	solo 5	S702	d/r	T205	d/r	TR401	e/r	off
Ralph	xb	Off	M104					
Luis	xb	Off						
Vacation		S	M	T	W	Th	F	S
Off Driver	Coverage	R#	R#	R#	R#	R#	R#	R#
Jimmy B.	Tommy	Off	M101	d/r	WD303	d/r	F505	d/r
Freddie F.	Michael	S702	d/r	T205	d/r	TR401	e/r	off
PTO								
Brian	Ralph		M104					
Rob	Float					TR405		

ABOUT THE AUTHOR

Mr. Ackiss has spent most of his time in the field of transportation working in manufacturing and in grocery distribution center environments. He served primarily as a supervisor and transportation manager in different facilities handling situations where quick and speedy action was necessary to make sure the DC and transportation department were successful. While many of these ideas are common knowledge, he learned that there was very limited published material on the subject readily available to the field. He compiled this information so that the wheel does not have to be reinvented every time someone comes into a new job as a manager in the field of transportation. Mr. Ackiss holds a BA in History from East Carolina University, an MBA from the University of Phoenix, and various certificates in management, quality control, and transportation.

www.ingramcontent.com/pod-product-compliance
Lightning Source LLC
LaVergne TN
LVHW020006080526
838200LV00081B/4463